Seven Deadly Sins

&

Heavenly Virtues

Dwight Hairston Currence

First Original Edition

Copyright© 2023 by Dwight Hairston Currence

ISBN-979-8-9871031-3-5

Published by Simply Snowden

This book is my experience, except where noted otherwise. This is the male perspective and what I see through my eyes.

Some call them the seven deadly sins; others identify them as the seven evils humans must resist. I pray, I write for your interpretation.

Seven Deadly Sins

Table of Contents

Let's identify -

The Seven Deadly Sins and The Heavenly Virtues:

SINS	VIRTUES
LUST	CHASTITY
ENVY	KINDNESS
SLOTH	DILIGENCE
GREED	CHARITY
GLUTTONY	TEMPERENCE
WRATH	PATIENCE
PRIDE	HUMILITY

L U S T

Let's start with LUST.

According to the Merriam-Webster Online Dictionary, the definition of lust is usually intense or unbridled sexual desire.

WOW, now that's a very powerful word!

I started with lust because lust can confuse you. It's deceptive, attractive, and yet satisfying. Lust has the same job all sins have. They want you to crack the backdoor, open the window, or make you give up so they can control your thoughts. Lust is the gatekeeper that makes you feel like something is missing; you don't know what it is or cannot put a finger on it.

"Flee from sexual immorality. Every other sin a person commits is outside the body, but the sexually immoral person sins against his own body."

1 Corinthians   6:18   ESV

I start a typical day, go to work, get to the location, and then, Wham - There it is - it hits me square in the face! This lady is sitting behind a desk. She smiles at me, and I begin to feel like it is just for me. My thoughts start to take over, and I hear a sound in my head that says, "She wants you." Now I have become preoccupied with the belief that she wants me. All this happens in the 1.25 seconds of a smile. Lust has a way of filling a void or filling something missing in your life. Now at this point, desire has taken my mind off my job. I have the dangerous position of inspecting elevators, but Lust doesn't care about my job or the danger. My focus now is on choosing whether I want her or not. Lust has already convinced me that she wants me. Wow, this beast is selfish and egotistical! I'm naturally charming and charismatic, but this lady has no clue that all of these thoughts are being processed in my mind.

Lust strokes the ego to open the door for many other sins. Lust will convince you that you are more than what you are. Lust will make your body respond with chills and notions of premeditated sex. The adrenaline rush is her unexpected acceptance. The excitement comes from her unexpected touch. The satisfaction comes from her begging me.

Why does Lust take a stranger and convince me that she can't live without me?

Does Lust want to chase or be caught?

Lust doesn't want satisfaction because Lust can never be satisfied. Lust just wants you to move on to the next. You will always be running, and the problem is you are only running from yourself. Lust is a feeling you will always chase from someone you can never have - yourself.

"For all that is in the world-the desires of the flesh and the desires of the eyes and pride in possessions-is not from the Father but is from the world."

1 John 2:16 ESV

Does Lust send out vibes?

When someone smiles or looks into your eyes, can you feel it?

Is that flirting, temptation, or lust?

Can they be the same?

Flirting is to trifle with or toy with an idea. According to the online Merriam-Webster Thesaurus, Trifle is to act without a serious purpose; it may imply playfulness.

Do you really want to trifle with fire?

Are flirtatious thoughts one of those thoughts that the beast of lust controls?

The beast of lust has the other sins hiding behind it, and you can't see them because of flirting. Flirting has that warm and fuzzy feeling, that burst of dopamine, and that void you need to fill. Flirting is on the Beast of Lust's payroll. Flirting gets paid in full when Lust controls your thoughts. One bad thought can be an opportunity for Lust to control your every thought only to give them away freely to evil actions.

Okay, get ready for this - there are no good or bad thoughts. It's when you let the thoughts hang around for too long that it is bad; it cracks the door, and then here ego comes. So, let's talk about what to do with the thoughts. When a thought enters your mind, you must accept it and process it. Accepting it means understanding the thought's motive, consequences, and actions. Process means to decide, act on it, and let it go. I'm going to say that again, *"Let it go."* If you don't let thoughts go and move on, they will only hang around. Then you start waiting on another thought, and it gains power and cracks the back door or window to keep you running inside your mind.

That leads me to the word temptation. According to the online Google Dictionary, temptation is the desire to do something wrong or unwise; something or a course of action that allures or entices. There I did it; I opened a can of worms. Enticement can mean to lure, and allurement can be tempting and seem irresistible.

How does Lust push temptation out front to do the dirty work?

Do I really need to answer that?

Temptation can be summed up in one word ... BAIT. According to Collins Online Dictionary, to bait means to lure by deception or trickery so you can destroy or entrap. I don't know about you, but I need a break after that one. Thoughts entered my mind of past temptations that weren't good for me. The crazy thing is, I now know lust was the kingpin. Today, I can process the thoughts that just entered my mind and let them go.

"No temptation has overtaken you that is not common to man. G.O.D. is faithful, and he will not let you be tempted beyond your ability, but with the temptation, he will also provide the way of escape, that you may be able to endure it."

1   Corinthians   10:13   ESV

During my typical day, I encounter many women. The ones who have the beast of lust on them have radar. It's also called "having game". They see you before you see them, they set a trap, and then you walk through the door. The energy is so thick you can cut it with a knife. I can feel her undressing me with her eyes. I can see her heartbeat increase. She licks her lips with a smile when I notice her. She stands up to make sure I notice her silhouette.

Lust is a liar!

Women, do you sometimes dress provocatively to flirt, tempt, or just bait?

I'm not saying I haven't put on a tank top to stroke my ego because I'm diesel, and I know this. I don't make the rules or understand why there are two sets of rules for men and women, known as a double standard.

Spoiler alert: to the women, if a lot of your body is exposed, men think you have the beast of lust on you. I'm just being 100 percent honest with you. I am in no way or shape saying that men have the right to act on any feeling they have because of how a woman chooses to dress.

It's three a. m. in the morning, I've wanted to give it to her, and now it's my turn. I want to ensure she remembers it for the rest of her life. I let out a scream when I rolled over and hit the floor. I woke up to find it was only a dream. While I was sleeping, the beast of lust was trying to crack the back door for the other sins to move in.

Lust has your best friend and your worst enemy also on the payroll. Pleasure can lure you in with someone you just met or broke up with that you know wasn't good for you. Pleasure is plain and straightforward – its gratification.

How in the world can pleasure move in if you are sleeping?

Okay, do you remember your thoughts?

They turn your mind into a condominium if you don't accept and process a thought. Check out my book, MY

TRUTH: JUST CARE. I explain the condominium theory and the C.A.R.E. method. If it doesn't make sense to you that you are under attack while sleeping, keep reading.

How can you defend yourself from your thoughts?

They say it takes 66 days to start a habit, on average, but how long does it take to really break one?

Have you always held on to thoughts that didn't matter? Some call them resentments.

How do you know if you process the thought correctly?

Are you making this difficult?

Wake up in the morning and start with positive thoughts. One way is to make a gratitude list. I know you have things that have gone well in your life, and you are in control of your thoughts and attack your positive or negative day; you pick.

You must process your thoughts for motive, consequences, and actions. You must decide, act on it, and let go. There will be mistakes along the way. Move on; it's okay. The more practice you get, the more confident you will get in processing a thought. You want to get to the point of C.A.R.E..

Clear your mind, Accept God, Reap what you sow, and Enjoy the ride.

"But I say to you that everyone who looks at women with lustful intent has already committed adultery with her in his heart."

Matthew   5:28   ESV

CHASTITY

Chastity is the state or practice of refraining from extramarital, or from all, sexual intercourse, and a celibate is a person who refrains from marriage and sexual relations, according to an online dictionary. Many people like to use monks as an example of a celibate, and more often than not, being celibate is for religious reasons. However, not everyone defines celibacy the same. Some abstain from all kinds of sexual contact, even holding hands, while others only refrain from sexual intercourse.

"For this is the will of God, your sanctification: that you abstain from sexual immorality."

1   Thessalonians   4:3   ESV

I never thought that I would be able to say I was celibate for over six years. Refraining from sex was easy while I cared for my mom when she was ill; she stayed with me full-time, and I didn't have the time or energy to date anyway. Although, I did change some learned behaviors to take the temptation out of my thoughts, like the television shows I watched. I reverted to watching old television shows; they did not have sex and nudity like some shows today.

Let's get to the root of the problem. I didn't have a healthy thought process, and I let my sense of sight, smell, and touch control my actions. I let thoughts hang around inside my mind until they became terrible actions.

All my life, women have held the power of sex over my head, going back to my teenage years. I went into more detail in my book, *My Truth, Ten Words, Ten Days.* As my faith got stronger, I took my power back, saying I must get to know the person first. It didn't take courage; it took faith.

I was astonished at the women who lead with their bodies. I wouldn't be able to see it if I hadn't built my faith and realized that lust was taking over. Women, sex isn't your lottery ticket; it's your hidden treasure. Not necessarily to be hidden from everyone, but exposed to the right one, exposed to your husband. Back in the day, people refrained from sex until they were married for a reason. Sex muddies the waters when getting to know someone. Being celibate has changed my life and how I approach sex and intimacy. It has given me an added source of confidence, knowing that I don't have the beast of lust on me.

Monogamy comes to mind when thinking about chastity. Monogamy is the state or practice of having only one sexual partner at a time, the state or custom of being married to only one person at a time, or the practice of having a single mate during a period of time, according to the Merriam -Webster Online Dictionary. However, monogamous relationships can be sexual or emotional, but it's usually both. Essentially, monogamous relationships are being loyal and faithful to one person. While some people think it is okay to text others provocatively, others believe it's okay to have those same thoughts about someone.

No, no, and no!

You are developing a learned behavior for making bad decisions — enough of that. I will not say anything else about chastity because it speaks for itself. You know right from wrong.

"For God gave us a spirit, not of fear but power and love and self-control."

2 Timothy 1:7 ESV

ENVY

Just the word envy sounds like you should stay away from it. According to the online dictionary, envy, as a noun, is a feeling of discontented or resentful longing aroused by someone else's possessions, qualities, or luck. Using envy as a verb, like when you envy someone, you desire a quality, a possession, or a desirable attribute belonging to someone else.

After Lust cracks the back door, the beast of Envy is the first one that comes in. Lust and Envy keep you chasing the one thing you will never catch - yourself. Envy drives you to desire but can't touch. Envy obliterates your success, only to serve you a hefty dose of defeat. Using the law of gravity, pulling you down is easier than picking you up. The green-eyed monster's mask can only be seen when you open your mouth, tempting you with people, places, and things. You can't hide from the words that come out of your mouth.

Jealousy, another word that sounds like trouble, comes to my mind when I hear the word envy. With no lasting power, the bodyguard for Envy zaps you when you see a car you want, a bigger house than yours, better teeth, curly hair, a better body, more money, on vacation in Hawaii, or just something you like or want. The zap reminds you that Envy is the boss.

"For where jealousy and selfish ambition exist, there will be disorder and every vile practice."

James   3:16   ESV

Envy hired two managers, Prejudiced and Hateful. I struggled as a child with intolerance. Being light-skinned and having curly hair constantly reminded me that I didn't really fit in. I was a victim of hate from both sides of the coin.

I envied my friends who just had what you would call a normal life. Even though some of my friends struggled with having food or clothing, they knew who they were. I thought they were lucky to have such minuscule problems because I always felt I didn't fit in or know my identity. On the flip side, they could have been just as envious of me not having any problems with having food or clothing. Envy doesn't discriminate; it can take control of anyone.

Prejudice is just a loyal manager for Envy. Prejudice is a disease that cuts so deep it runs into your bloodstream. You come into the world and are taught by your parents, often with prejudices. Those prejudices put blinders on your eyes to judge people based on what *you* see or have been taught. Confused with my identity, I would judge dark-skinned people the way the media portrayed them on the news, which was not fair to them or me.

"Judge not, that you may be judged. For with the judgment you pronounce you will be judged, and with the measure you use it will be measured to you. Why do you see a speck that is in your brother's eye, but do not notice the log that is in your own eye? Or how can you say to your brother, Let me take the speck out of your eye,' when there is the log in your own eye? You hypocrite, first take the log out of your own eye, and then you will see clearly to take the speck out of your brother's eye."

Matthew 7:1-5   ESV

How can you be prejudiced towards someone if you feel you are better than them?

You have an unfavorable opinion based on a learned behavior taught to you. Prejudice has gasoline called preconception and bigotry that fuels Envy to keep you wanting more and more preconceptions and bigotry. You probably have noticed that gasoline prices always get higher when there is a catastrophe, leading to much more devastation than already exists, which makes no sense.

"There is neither Jew nor Greek, there is neither slave nor free, there is no male and female, for you are all one in Christ Jesus."

Galatians   3:28   ESV

According to the online dictionary, hatred is a severe or intense dislike. Like all great managers, Hatred does its job well. Hate is a blend of emotions, mostly anger, disgust, or contempt. This emotion often triggers destructive behaviors, with animosity and acrimony. There are no levels of hate because it is the opposite of love.

"If anyone says, "I love God," and hates his brother, he is a liar; for he who does not love his brother whom he has seen cannot love God whom he has not seen."

1 John   4:20   ESV

How can you hate someone so much if you know nothing about that person?

"The one who conceals hatred has lying lips, and whoever utters slander is a fool."

Proverbs   10:18   ESV

People will often say that they hate traffic jams, waiting in line, a particular food, etc. When someone hates another person, usually, it is aimed at the person's behavior and not necessarily the person. However, when a person's emotions get more intense than being angry with a person's behavior, it transforms into hate. Hatred is like anger on steroids. Hatred is like a feeling of rage that can only be scratched by acting out on someone. Hate's goal is not to change the person's behavior; it's to eliminate the target altogether, with the perception that the behavior is unchangeable and bad.

Hatred plays on triggered emotions that cause many actions and reactions based on stereotypes and looks.

How often are you standing in line, and a person who looks different from you is standing behind you, making you feel very uncomfortable?

I know you can say that isn't extreme dislike. That person could be a doctor, lawyer, teacher, nurse, or just someone in line. It takes a toll if someone is always looking at you like you are a threat.

Why do they have to be judged by the way they look?

Animosity is an extreme dislike, with the action of acrimony or wrath, that leads to malevolent behavior.

When someone shows hatred toward someone, why follow up with acrimony?

Words most times cut deeper than a knife.

If Hatred works for Envy, what are you envious of?

Hatred is the only emotion that you can explain behind closed doors with your kids.

Spoiler alert: teach your children that love is stronger than hate if you want to end hatred.

"There are six things that the Lord hates, seven that are an abomination to him: haughty eyes, a lying tongue, and hands that shed innocent blood, a heart that devises wicked plans, feet that make haste to run to evil, a false witness who breathes out lies, and one who sow discord among brothers."

Proverbs   6:16-19   ESV

KINDNESS

Kindness ... sounds angelic - it is doing a good act, favor, or behavior to someone else. Part of the Fruit of the Spirit, kindness is being merciful, showing tenderness and friendliness, being sweet, generous, and considerate, among many other words that would describe kindness. But most of all, to know the meaning of kindness is to know Jesus; He was the epitome of kindness.

FLASHBACK - In 1978, I remember studying for the S.A.T. The two words that seemed to come up all the time were benevolence and countenance. To this day, I love sliding those words into a conversation to watch a person's countenance. Benevolent means wanting to help others, and countenance means facial expressions.

"Be kind to one another, tenderhearted, and forgiving one another, as God in Christ forgave you."

Ephesians   4:32   ESV

"A man who is kind benefits himself, but a cruel man hurts himself."

Proverbs   11:17   ESV

Kindness has an army of soldiers. I think of Courtesy as a colonel, Decency as the captain, and Sympathy as the lieutenant. According to the online dictionary, courtesy is being polite, respectful, or considerate; it is an adjective describing how someone acts. Decency is the showing of politeness in one's attitude, a behavior that conforms to acceptable standards of morality or respectability.

Finally, sympathy is the feelings of pity and sorrow for someone else's misfortune. All these are important in showing kindness to someone in a way that is needed for a particular time.

How do you define good manners?

Some say to treat people the way you want to be treated.

What if you are treating people the way you were taught?

Courtesy isn't about the way people treat you. Courtesy is about how you treat others. Please don't get caught up in thinking someone is not courteous to you because you deserve it. There are two types of angels, the ones to pick you up and the ones to pull you down. That person in the grocery line could be an angel trying to pick you up.

Driving in my car is another time I want people to show me courtesy. I don't understand where some people got their driver's licenses. It's so easy some mornings to get caught up in starting my day with someone cutting me off. It's even more aggravating in the afternoon going home. I have developed a phrase, "Thank you, Lord, I'm not in a hurry or late." My life is stress-free and filled with inner peace. I don't allow those angels to pull me down. Thank you, Lord.

How does the way people treat you affect you?

Do you retaliate?

Does their countenance get you?

What makes a decent person?

How do you treat others?

How do you rate your actions toward others?

Decency is recognizing a standard of good taste and doing the right thing. The sad part about the world is that most people associate decent people with not who they are but who they think they are. Social media plays such a significant role in the world today that you can portray a lie with just a few keystrokes.

I have chills right now thinking about a millionaire who helped charities. Nobody knew about it until he died; that is the definition of decency; to be a good person without glory or fame. All the glory and fame belong to God. If you are still trying to figure that out, no harm, no foul. I pray my perception of myself is worthy of God's presence.

Sympathy deals with emotions. Sympathy is the power of sharing another person's feelings.

Does sympathy get you caught up in feeling sorry for a person?

Is that kindness or sorrow?

Sorrow is grief. To me, sympathy is feelings of sorrow with emotions of understanding. Kindness is the showing of empathy and compassion.

Who should you help?

How do you decide?

Spoiler Alert: develop a relationship with GOD, and you don't have to make any decisions.

"Finally, all of you have unity of mind, sympathy, brotherly love, a tender heart, and a humble mind."

1 Peter 3:8 ESV

S L O T H

Sloth sounds horrible; it is pretty much laziness. Laziness tells you, you can take a day off, and Sloth wants you to drop your guard and buy into an every day off. That's how it starts; one day turns into two days and two into three. Sloth and laziness go hand in hand; it comes from learned behaviors - behaviors set up by others for your failure. Sloth is a fungus that grows in your mind; it chokes your ambition, robs your dreams, and has only one goal, to stop you from clarity.

"The hand of the diligent will rule, while the slothful will be put to forced labor."

Proverbs   12:24   ESV

Laziness slows down your heart, makes your feet feel like concrete, and teaches your mind to procrastinate. Sloth only has one sidekick, Procrastination, who is used to crack the back door in your thought process.

RECAP: thought process; When a thought enters your mind, you must accept it and process it. Accepting it means understanding the thought's motive, consequences, and actions. Process means to decide, act on it, and let it go.

Your healthy thought process dies when you procrastinate. It causes you to stuff your feelings and resentments inside. Procrastination sucks you in with the comfort of thinking you have a solution. The only problem is that it was not resolved; you only thought about it and didn't actually do anything. Procrastination closes the deal with, "deal with it later, not right now, or it's okay to wait." Procrastination has you running inside your mind to devise a solution; sometimes, it may take days, weeks, or even never. It is called renting space in your mind for free. You do it to yourself, so stop procrastinating! Procrastination has one job to control your thought process. I know I'm beating a dead horse, but sloth is sneaky; it uses phrases like, *there's always tomorrow, it's not that serious*, or the one I love the most, *don't worry, I got it.* The problem is YOU don't get it. That leads me to Sloth's paid hit-man.

Who do you think that is?

One guess! Come on!

You got it ... lying

Lying is what lazy people do to cover up their laziness.

Do you hear the words coming from my mouth?

When Procrastination doesn't get you, Sloth takes a hit out on you, with yourself. Sloth is insidious and convinces you that it can be done later, and sometimes that subsequently does not get there. This process leads to a lie you might have to tell to cover for yourself. You lie for not cleaning up your house, paying a bill, or anything that requires you to put forth an effort.

WOW - did you hear what I said?

Put forth an effort! Because the lies you build brick by brick close in on you because no one can trust you.

I wonder why?

Because you are a liar, the sad part is, it has become your standard, and everybody around you knows. You begin to believe your lies. Let's not forget Sloth chokes your ambition and robs you of your dreams. I could probably go on and on, but if it doesn't make sense to you, reread what sloth can do to you if you let it.

"The sluggard does not plow in the autumn; he will seek at harvest and have nothing."

Proverbs   20:4   ESV

"Look carefully then how you walk, not as unwise but as wise, making the best use of the time, because the days are evil. Therefore do not be foolish, but understand what the will of the Lord is."

Ephesians   5:15-17   ESV

"The hand of the diligent will rule, while the slothful will be put to forced labor."

Proverbs   12:24   ESV

DILIGENCE

The online dictionary states that the word diligence is an earnest and constant effort. It is a careful and persistent exertion of mind and body, and it takes perseverance to complete an action set in motion. It's amazing how words sound so powerful.

Diligence has two brothers and one sister for help. The first brother is Intensity. Intensity is passion and force, and the intensity of achieving goals gives you the passion and desire to have the faith to keep going.

It was just nine months ago when I started writing my first book. Now I'm finishing up book number 3 and working on book number 4. I give all the glory to God. Because Diligence, and his brother, Intensity, continue to drive me to keep writing despite the setback with my first. Sometimes you may have obstacles that seem to get in your way, like my book, *My Truth: Ten Days Ten Words,* taking longer to publish than I wanted. Despite the obstacles I had to overcome, I felt a force that compelled me to let God handle the process and do what I do - just write. To write what the Holy Spirit has inspired me to write. Intensity kept empowering me to keep moving forward

Diligence's younger brother, Quickness, or you can call him Swiftness. Quickness can be a crutch if you move too fast. I can remember being younger and having the dexterity with coordination to be swift. I could go non-stop all day, not even thinking about lunch. That's why Quickness is the younger brother. I use my quickness now with my mind to take fewer steps and take more time to plan while finishing the task simultaneously. It has changed from a physical quickness to a mental quickness. I encourage young people to plan more. You will finish quicker. Quickness for me today means getting it done faster, going in a straight line. A straight line is the shortest distance between two points.

You have to always keep in mind that Sloth and Diligence are cousins, and they communicate pretty often. Once you start something, Sloth always knows about it and wants to slow you down, never wanting you to finish.

Stay on track with Intensity and Quickness, and their little sister, Alertness; her nickname is Baby Girl. Alertness is being fully aware, wide awake, and swift. Baby Girl has that maternal instinct to nurture. Baby Girl sends warning signs to her brothers that procrastination is trying to creep in the back door.

All families who have a healthy relationship have alertness. You want the best for each other, and the only way you can receive your blessings is to have a healthy relationship with them. Each family member has a role, and you must let God show you their role. We only see with our eyes, but God wants us to see what He sees.

I have family members that I try to avoid, but on my spiritual journey, God revealed to me that sometimes I need to be reminded by others. I try to encourage them through my testimony of what God has done for me. Although I don't have to spend much time around them, staying away altogether is a form of fear, a fear of what they might say to me or judge me.

Fear and Faith don't live in the same house. Diligence and sloth are like fear and faith; you will only have one or the other, and they don't thrive together. I challenge everyone who has been avoiding someone to get closure and resolve the issue.

"A slack hand causes poverty, but the hand of the diligent makes rich."

Proverbs   10:4   ESV

"The soul of the sluggard craves and get nothing, while the soul of the diligent is richly supplied."

Proverbs   13:4   ESV

"Only take care, and keep your soul diligently, lest you forget the things that your eyes have seen, and lest they depart from your heart all the days of your life. Make them known to your children and your children's children-"

Deuteronomy   4:9   ESV

"Keep your heart with vigilance, for from it flow the springs of life."

Proverbs   4:23   ESV

"The plans of the diligent lead surely to abundance, but everyone who is hasty comes only to poverty."

Proverbs   21:5   ESV

G R E E D

G R E E D ... What is greed?

Who is Greed?

I'll let you in on something most people don't know. Greed and Gluttony are twins, and I'll snitch on Gluttony later. The online dictionary states that greed is an intense and selfish desire for something, especially wealth, power, or food, or is an overwhelming desire to want more possessions. Gluttony is the one who pushes Greed to double-team you to open the back door, so they both can come in. Greed is so selfish that only one spirit gets along with him. You guessed it - selfishness. Selfishness is self-regard or egotism.

If I asked ten people if they were greedy, they would probably say *no*. If I gave those same people ten million dollars, they would probably show how greedy they are with their actions. Greed has a way of convincing you that you need something right here, right now, and it doesn't matter who you hurt or whether you can afford it.

My grandmother always said, "I've never seen anybody take a house or a car to heaven." Greed wants to drive your goals, drive your desires, and drive you right off a cliff. Greed will try to light a fire in your soul with only one purpose to burn down the inner lining of your heart. Greed wants you to have all the bells and whistles, only to lose your soul.

Greed is so hungry it feeds you with other people's accomplishments, not yours. Greed always wants you to look at what they have and ask yourself, *why don't I have that?*

I had three marriages and walked away from everything we had built together. The funny thing is - I had a conversation with one of my family members, and she told me I hadn't done anything, and my wives did it all. At that moment, Greed wanted to jump in and defend me; Greed wanted to take full credit for everything they now had, that it was all because of me. However, I know I was just bitter and wanted something, even if it was merely the credit for everything they now had.

Wow! Greed works by any means. You would think she would give me credit for something - not. Greed is just toxic, and greedy people just don't get it. Greedy people believe the one who gets the house and the car wins.

I used to think that materialistic things measured my accomplishments, but I now know they can become idols. Today, I enjoy the journey more than the reward. Greedy people don't know Envy is pushing them in the back. Greed puts you in a tunnel with a light you can see but never touch. Greed wants you to chase things for yourself instead of sharing the things with the people you love. My grandmother would always say, "You can chase the riches of the world, but you will lose your soul."

"But those who desire to be rich fall into temptation, into a snare, into many senseless and harmful desires that plunge people into ruin and destruction. For the love of money is a root of all kinds of evils. It is through this craving, some have wandered away from the faith and pierced themselves with many pangs."

1 Timothy   6:9-10   ESV

"And in their greed they will exploit you with false words. Their condemnation from long ago is not idle, and their destruction is not asleep."

2 Peter   2:3

"For what does it profit a man to gain the whole world and forfeit his soul?"

Mark   8:36   ESV

CHARITY

Charity is the sound you hear; it's the generous donations and actions to help the poor, helpless, or ill. My grandmother used to say, "charity starts at home." If you didn't learn to help others from your parents, then now is the time to start.

Spoiler alert: you should help people who need and want help.

You don't have to decide who is good or bad. God will make the right choice. You must build a relationship with God daily, and everything else will fall into place.

Charity feeds your soul and is a feeling you can only enjoy with a clean heart. It is not charity if you are riding dirty, selfish, or ego-driven while doing a good deed.

How do I know if it's charity?

Answer these three questions.

If I had only one dollar left, would I give it to a person in need?

Do I help people and then regret them doing nothing for me?

When I see a person begging for money, do I feel they are lazy and don't want to work?

What are your results?

Did you pass?

I don't know, did you?

If you want the results, talk to God. God has the answers to all your questions. God will provide clarity, inner peace, and freedom from self. Charity is like plugging into an electrical socket in the wall. The electricity will recharge you with faith, hope, and understanding. The faith you get in charity will strengthen your relationship with God.

In all things I have shown you that by working hard in this way we must help the weak and remember the words of the Lord Jesus, how he himself said, "It is more blessed to give than to receive."

Acts   20:35   ESV

"Do not neglect to do good and to share what you have, for such sacrifices are pleasing to God."

Hebrews   13:16   ESV

"Give, and it will be given to you. Good measure, pressed down, shaken together, running over, will be put into your lap. For with the measure you use it will be measured back to you."

Luke   6:38   ESV

"Whoever is generous to the poor lends to the LORD, and he will repay him for his deed."

Proverbs   19:17   ESV

GLUTTONY

St. Thomas Aquinas, a Dominican priest and Scriptural theologian, defines gluttony as an inordinate relationship with material things. [1] Primarily associated with habitual greed or excess in eating and drinking; and ingratitude for the goods we possess. I already told you Gluttony and Greed are twins. Gluttony takes obsession to a new level. Gluttony controls your thoughts to continue bodily harm. It tells you to keep eating, keep eating, keep eating. Gluttony brings the comfort of food as your safety blanket. It doesn't matter if you are hungry, it doesn't matter if you are alone, it doesn't matter if you have problems. Gluttony uses food to make you feel better. The only problem is Gluttony tells you that the more you eat, the better you will feel.

That's a lie! You might have that feeling at first, but that feeling of comfort is only brief. Then you find yourself eating more and more, and overeating makes you put on the pounds. As you put on the pounds, it starts to destroy your self-worth. The bigger you get, the smaller you feel.

Gluttony has two paid hitmen available at all times, Excess and Audacity. Excess and Audacity will lock in whenever you try to pull away from the table. Excess and Audacity use reverse psychology to convince you that you

---

[1] Saint Mary Catholic Church. *The Seven Deadly Sins: Gluttony.* 2023. https://stmaryrockledge.org/the-seven-deadly-sins-gluttony/#:~:text=Thomas%20Aquinas%20defines%20gluttony%20as,ultimate%20end%20of%20our%20lives. 2023.

want more and more. Yes, it sounds like greed; the only difference is Greed tells you that you need more and more. Gluttony tells you that you want more and more. That's why they are twins; they try to satisfy your wants and needs.

Spoiler alert: God provides all your needs.

Excess is an amount of something that is more than necessary or an extreme amount. Excess makes you believe that you only ate one bag of chips, but it was family-size. You begin to make excuses for hiding your eating. You begin to have bad health and lonely days and nights. *Excess* makes you feel like you can't live without it. The reverse psychology that Excess uses can be your worst nightmare.

Audacity is a shameless and bold disregard for others or your safety. Audacity uses reverse psychology, just like Excess. Audacity can convince you that alcohol is safe, even in excess, because it can make you feel good. Although, it actually numbs you, so you don't feel at all.

Audacity flips the script with cowardly guts and liquid courage. Audacity empowers alcohol in your system with no disregard for your recklessness. Audacity gives you the strength to take risks. Audacity sings a song in your mind,

> *"Don't stop; drink it, drink it! Don't stop; drink it, drink it!"*

If you hear this song, then you need help. Start by looking at yourself in the mirror. Love is greater than pain, hunger, or fear. God is always with you. We leave God; God never leaves us.

If you have received a D.U.I. or D.W.I., stop drinking alcohol. That was a cry for help. Go to a treatment center, and knock the door down. God's eyes are on the sparrow, and I know He watches me. Don't let this song be the last one you hear.

> *"Don't stop; drink it, drink it! Don't stop; drink it, drink it!"*

Get help now.

"But put on the Lord Jesus Christ, and make no provision for the flesh, to gratify its desires."

Romans   13:14   ESV

"They tested God in their heart by demanding the food they craved."

Psalm   78:18   ESV

"Their end is destruction, their God is their belly, and they glory in their shame, with minds set on earthly things."

Phillippians   3:19   ESV

"Or do you know that your body is a temple of the Holy Spirit within you, whom you have from God? You are not your own,"

1 Corinthians   6:19   ESV

TEMPERANCE

According to the online dictionary, Temperance is the quality of moderation or self-restraint; it is also abstinence from alcoholic drink

Does self-control mean you must trust yourself?

I have realized that I was my biggest problem. I used to run around inside my mind non-stop. I believe to have total temperance, you must have faith. Faith is a power that is greater than yourself. My faith in God has allowed me to enjoy inner peace, freedom, and temperance. God enables me to understand self-control and its importance.

There is a new word you should learn; it comes from self-control, God-control. Because this is a word I just made up, let me define it for you. The more you trust God, the more you trust his outcome. God-control allows you to stop worrying. God-control enables you to have inner peace every second of every day. God-control allows you to have freedom from self.

Self-control has a hidden agenda, people - the keyword is control. I'll say it again the keyword is CONTROL. I know some people will disagree with me. I'm not saying you shouldn't have self-control. I'm saying your faith should feed your self-control.

We are all human and sometimes fall short; however, strengthening your faith will feed your spirit, which will improve your self-control. Restraining your emotions, actions, and desires to be in harmony with the will of God will strengthen your relationship with Him. The big difference is getting up every morning and feeling like you are starting over every day versus getting up and feeling like you are growing stronger every day.

If you don't understand that having self-control is faith driven, you must pray for understanding. Self-control is like a battery; it will run down and go dead. Plug up to God-control, as He is an endless source of power. Feeding your faith is fuel for temperance. Just like God-control builds your confidence and self-esteem. Temperance is designed to build you up. You have only one requirement - faith in God.

"For God gave us a spirit not of fear but of power and love and self-control."

2 Timothy 1:7 ESV

"But I say, walk by the spirit, and you will not gratify the desires of the flesh."

Galatians 5:16 ESV

"If you have honey, eat only enough for you, lest you have your fill of it and vomit it."

Proverbs 25:16 ESV

WRATH

Merriam-Webster Online Dictionary defines wrath as strong vengeful anger or indignation; retributory punishment for an offense or a crime; divine chastisement

Why are we talking about anger?

During my experience dealing with angry people, they feel they aren't angry, that it's just their normal. Anger is hard to get out of your bloodstream and triggers irritation, rage, and resentment. Irritation is an emotion; it's the flint that starts the fire. Anger always reminds irritation that you just need to get it started. People only treat you the way you allow yourself to be treated.

If you put expectations on people, it only sets you up for disappointment. I can relate to being angry with people who didn't know I was displeased or irritated with them. This usually happened when I had an expectation of them, and they didn't fulfill that expectation. So when using expectations, only put the expectation on yourself.

Irritation also taps into your adrenaline, and it gives you a boost of dopamine that feels good. The only problem is that it is just an appetizer. Sometimes, it doesn't stop until you have kicked into full-blown rage mode. Rage mode is when someone has pissed you off, disrespected you, or done you severely wrong.

Spoiler alert: in most cases, they don't have a clue that they have set you off.

You have often conjured all this wrongdoing up in your mind, and now the rage is in effect because they responded. Rage is violent, uncontrollable anger that has your heart beating so loud you can hear it, causing a feeling like you to have to defend yourself when you are the one who started it. When you have rage, you have no self-control. If and only if you can get past the anger, you have resentment waiting on you.

I explain resentments in my book, *MY TRUTH: JUST CARE.* Resentments take up space in your mind. They move in and call it their condominium, and they call it their condominium because they are territorial and take ownership.

The resentments live because of the irritation, which is the match that lights the rage, the fire. The resentment is the wax that keeps it burning, and if you don't resolve the issue, that wax will be there waiting to be lit again with a slight irritation. Let it go, and let God. Live in the moment.

Please don't fall into the wrath; it wants you to self-destruct. First, you start destroying the relationships around you, cutting ties with loved ones, and then building walls of isolation. This behavior only leads to a bad ending, so get back to the thought process that helps you resolve those issues and move on.

When a thought enters your mind, you must accept it and process it. Accepting it means understanding the thought's motive, consequences, and actions. Processing means to decide, act on it, and let it go. Don't let wrath take control of your life.

Give that control over to God and let Him handle the wrath.

"Refrain from anger, and forsake wrath! Fret not yourself; it tends only to evil."

Psalm   37:8   ESV

"Beloved, never avenge yourselves, but leave it to the wrath of God, for it is written, "Vengeance is mine, I will repay, says the Lord."

Romans   12:19   ESV

"A soft answer turns away wrath, but a harsh word stirs up anger."

Proverbs   15:1   ESV

"Be not quick in your spirit to become angry, for anger lodges in the bosom of fools."

Ecclesiastes   7:9   ESV

"Be angry and do not sin; do not let the sun go down on your anger."

Ephesians   4:26   ESV

"Good sense makes one slow to anger, and it is in his glory to overlook the offense."

Proverbs   19:11   ESV

"A fool gives full vent to his spirit, but a wise man quietly holds back."

Proverbs   29:11   ESV

PATIENCE

Patience is a word that, if you don't know what it means, sounds peaceful. The online dictionary states that patience is the capacity to accept, tolerate, or suffer without losing temper or irritation. When they came up with the word patience, they started with the word peace, and the letters are in it for a reason. Peace is not hard to come by when you have patience, and having inner peace is priceless.

Usually, as I am waiting in line at the grocery store and someone is waiting on a price check or deciding what to put back because they don't have enough money, I think of my mom and what she taught me. I was very blessed growing up that I didn't worry about how to pay for the things I wanted and needed, but my mom taught me that you should never be above picking up a penny.

My mom always found pennies on the ground when we were shopping. It was a lesson in humility as well as patience. Sometimes, picking the penny up off the ground was hard, and I would want to give up, but she always insisted that I pick it up. So, when I finally got the penny in my hand, it felt like a million bucks. It's now a feeling that calms my heart.

Patience is good until you run out of it; then, it is a flip-flopper. The only good feeling that can crack the door to a bad feeling; it's almost like Wrath hides behind Patience to sneak in the door. The sad thing about Patience is it can only last as long as Anger allows. Anger reminds me of the candles on my birthday cake that you blow out but come backlit, ready to blow out again. At first, it's a great joke, but when your patience runs out, it leaves you angry, especially when everyone is laughing.

Wrath knows it is just a matter of time before you lose patience. That's why you must continue to feed your spirit so inner peace can grow. It is the extended version of patience.

Patience is the opposite of wrath. As wrath has irritation, patience is on a timer. Wrath has rage, and patience has inner peace. Wrath has resentments, and patience has forgiveness.

I have one question for you.

How do you use the time you save running from point A to point B?

Patience is designed to slow you down from harming yourself and is a defense mechanism for survival.

Why do you think most older people move slowly?

Okay, never mind.

How about the number of mistakes you make in a hurry?

Okay, forget about that one too. The last one, going too fast on the road, can get you a speeding ticket. You get the point. You must slow down long enough to hear the beat of your heart with others. I want to make sure you heard me the first time. Patience is a flip-flopper. You can explode within your mind. Get out of your own way. Patience is the emotion that requires climate control. You always want to remain in the cool regions.

"Rejoice in hope, be patient in tribulation, be constant in prayer."

Romans   12:12   ESV

"Love is patient and kind; love does not envy or boast; it is arrogant."

1   Corinthians   13:4

"Be still before the Lord and wait patiently for him; fret not yourself over the one who prospers in his own way, over the man who carries out evil devices!"

Psalm   37:7   ESV

"Be patient, therefore, brothers, until the coming of the Lord. See how the farmer waits for the precious fruit of the earth, being patient about it, until it receives the early and late rains."

James   5:7   ESV

"You also, bc paticnt. Establish your hearts, for the coming of the Lord is at hand."

James   5:8   ESV

"But the one who endures to the end will be saved."

Matthew   24:13   ESV

PRIDE

I don't even know how to attack pride; pride is a double-edged sword. Pride can be good and bad, depending on how you use it. Pride is too high an opinion of one's ability or worth, or it could be a feeling of satisfaction and pleasure from one's achievements. It's okay to feel a sense of pride in something you do or achieve; however, when that pride turns to arrogance, that is when it crosses the line.

Let's get real - as pride arises from taking responsibility for a specific action that might be considered socially valued and positive, arrogance arises from pride not in one's actions but in one's "global self," having an overbearing pride and confidence in one's self.

I was single for five years and dated myself; I did this for many reasons. There's no way I would not have dated myself before that time because not only was I told I was arrogant, but I was arrogant and needed to change. I'm humbled today to be able to look in the mirror and not at the mirror. Now let's not get it twisted.

Growing up with my grandparents, I heard, "Take pride in your work. The only thing you have is your name and your word." Hearing that led me to integrity—this word was drilled into my head. I don't think many young people today have heard the term integrity, and it's not their fault. Integrity is honesty with strong ethical and moral principles even when no one is watching. Having integrity is taking pride in everything you do; it shows your character. At least, that is what I was taught.

In 2020, pride became a big racial word and a source of social friction. I look at the issues today with pride and see that being prideful can lead to self-destruction. When you start feeling the need to live up to others' expectations by taking credit for things that are not yours, lying, and cheating to make others see you the way you want to feel. Pride leads to hubris, the opposite of humility. That type of pride is usually driven by poor self-worth and shame and compensates for that by feeling superior. This feeling then leads to looking for the flaws in others and criticizing others as a defense for their own insecurities and shortcomings. Pride is the type of beast that chokes you until you don't care. Pride takes arrogance and puts blinders on you like a horse, and you become narrow-minded and stop growing. Don't cross the thin line between arrogance and confidence. If someone tells you you are arrogant, look at yourself and find humility.

"When pride comes, then comes disgrace, but with the humble is wisdom."

Proverbs   11:2   ESV

For the wicked boasts of the desires of his soul, and the one greedy for gain curses and renounces the Lord. In the Pride of his face, the wicked does not seek him; all his thought are, "There is no God."

Psalm   10:3-4   ESV

But he gives more grace. Therefore it says, "God opposes the proud, but gives grace to the humble."

James   4:6   ESV

"Everyone who is arrogant in heart is an abomination to the Lord; be assured, he will not go unpunished."

Proverbs   16:5   ESV

"For if anyone thinks he is something, when he is nothing, he deceives himself."

Galatians   6:3   ESV

HUMILITY

How do you take a word with so much power and try to interpret it?

How do I handle this word and make you understand it?

How do I take humility and make you feel it?

It's no secret that I have been ego-driven most of my life, and I'm grateful I don't have that beast on me anymore. Merriam-Webster Online Dictionary says that humility is the freedom from pride or arrogance, the quality or state of being. I start my day off with a gratitude list. It humbles me how God has brought me a mighty long way. I tried all my life to do things my way.

Spoiler alert: it doesn't work - God provides all your needs.

I spent my life going after my wants. God's needs are much greater than my wants. God has me doing pull-ups (the work). I look at little children having so much humility. Sometimes the more they grow, the less humble they become. On the flip side, I look at older people as having so much humility. The life experience between those times is what I want to focus on. Humility is needed in every aspect of your life, even with the seven deadly sins and the heavenly virtues.

How does this work?

When the Beast of Lust is trying to crack the back door, stop him in his tracks and let out a scream. "Lust, leave me alone. God, please humble me." You must humble yourself to trust God. Remember, Lust uses flirting and temptation to get you hooked. Humility has a cold bucket of water ready for you. If you hold it close, humility will give you a warmer and fuzzier feeling, stronger than lust. Lust is in your mind, and humility is in your heart. Let go and let God. "Lord, please clean my heart from lust. Humble me to do your will. I give you all the praise and glory. In Jesus's name, Amen."

Why do you need humility with chastity?

If you stroke your ego believing you are celibate because you got this. It's just a matter of time before your ego turns against you. That's my story, and I'm sticking to it. Some people only call on God when there is trouble, but you must also praise him during good times. Giving God the glory quiets the voice of your ego. "God, thank you for keeping me celibate. In Jesus's name, Amen."

Envy is very tricky. You may have the beast of envy on you and don't even know it. Some people have been taught and are controlled by prejudice and hate. People doubted that you would read my book; I am talking about the people closest to me, like family, friends, co-workers, etc. Take baby steps by adding doubters to your prayer list. Remember, you must be specific about what you are praying for. "Lord, please clean my family, friends, and co-workers' hearts from prejudice, hatred, and envy. Please, God, humble them to hear your voice and know it is you, God. In Jesus's name, Amen."

Kindness is a learned behavior, and kindness feeds your spirit. The funny thing is kindness is a twin. I can be in line in the grocery store, and I see a person with a hand full of groceries holding on. I hear kindness say, "Let them go ahead of you." Another voice said, "They should have gotten a buggy."

Spoiler alert: the other voice isn't kindness. "Lord, please fill my heart with courtesy, decency, sympathy, and kindness. Lord, please keep me humble to do your will. In Jesus's name, Amen."

Sloth grows out of control and lives in a mess. Sloth whispers in both ears, "This isn't a mess." The problem is those whispers are not reality. Humility is the only way you can stop the whispering in your ears from laziness and procrastination. Humility will make you cry for no reason. Humility will change your learned bad behaviors. Humility will tear down the walls you have built all your life. Once the walls are down, the sunlight will shine for you to see the reality of that mess. "Lord, please clean my heart from laziness, procrastination, and sloth. Give me a clean heart so I may serve you. In Jesus's name, Amen."

Diligence can be overwhelming when you don't have humility. You can get in such a big hurry that you will miss your blessings. You cross paths with people who need you to be an angel to them. Naturally, you don't have time because you have to achieve your goal for that day. The only goal you should have is trying to make it to heaven. Diligence mixes with humility long enough for you to slow down to smell the roses. Stay on task and get it in. Humility gives you that balance to take your foot off the gas pedal. Humility feeds the spirit that makes you stronger. "Lord, please fill my heart with diligence. Lord, humble me to do your will. In Jesus's name, Amen."

Greed … every time I type this word, it makes me feel like something terrible is about to happen. Greed wants to live in your soul. Greed tempts you with wants. Learn the difference between God's needs and what you think you want. It's not for you to try to figure it out. Never question God. Always pray for understanding. "Lord, please deliver me from greed. Lord, please give me a clean heart so I may serve thee. In Jesus's name, Amen."

Charity starts at home. Charity is that warm cup of hot chocolate when snow is on the ground. You can feel the heat in the palms of your hands. You don't care for the snow but want that feeling of hot cocoa with it. Charity and humility have the same relationship. They get along together. The feeling of helping people in need is humbling. I try to pay for people who are behind me in line daily. The feeling always humbles me to see the look in their eyes. Humility reminds me that one person can make a difference. "Lord, please fill my heart with charity. I give you all the praise and glory. In Jesus's name, Amen."

Gluttony, oh gluttony! When I see people overeating, I pray because something is wrong or missing in their life.

Spoiler alert: it's GOD.

If you say gluttony, most people will say food.

How do you draw the line when you must eat to survive?

Can you hear me?

Change your eating habits, the type of food you eat, and the amount. I know, tell me something I don't know.

Spoiler alert: you must humble yourself to the fact that you have a problem that must be addressed.

I've heard people say: it runs in my family; I'm just big-boned. Yes, it probably does run in the family because, many times, issues are swept under the rug and not addressed. Humble yourself to your health. It's not healthy to not resolve problems that can affect your health. God is there for you. Be aware of the different types of gluttony that can control your life. Addictions can be gluttonous, like when you start drinking alcohol and can't stop. Today is the first day of the rest of your life. "Lord, please clean my heart of gluttony. May I hear your voice and know it's you, Lord. Please humble me to hear your voice. In Jesus's name, Amen."

Temperance is self-control, and you have to be careful with self-control. Remember the new word, God-Control. The thing about God-Control is it is an endless source of power. Plugging into God-Control takes a mountain and makes it look like a molehill. God-Control allows you to take one step back and two steps forward.

I know ...

How does humility fit in?

Get out of your own way. Let God control the outcome by trusting him. "Lord, please fill my heart with temperance to do your will. Please humble me. I trust God will control the outcome. In Jesus's name, Amen."

Wrath sounds like what the word means. To put out this fire starter, you must bring a firetruck. There's only one fireman needed to put out the fire. It is Humility. Humility can blow out the triggers of irritation, rage, and resentment. Irritation is an emotion, but humility is a stronger emotion. Irritation wants to start the fire, but Humility will blow out irritation and keep you calm forever. Wrath can be a life-threatening emotion. Wrath will pull you deeper and deeper into a self-made pit in your mind. The ladder that you can use to get out is humility. This ladder is always within reach. Wrath knows it doesn't stand a chance because Humility will never leave you behind. "Lord, please deliver me from wrath. Lord, please clean my heart. If there is anything there not worthy of your presence, please remove it. In Jesus's name, Amen."

Patience started with the word peace in it. You will never have patience without peace.

How do you get peace?

Glad you asked … humility. You must humble yourself to a power that is greater than yourself. I call my greater power God. God gives me inner peace and freedom of self because I trust and love him. It's hard to put into words because it is a feeling. I'm humbled every time I hear his voice with patience. I sometimes want God to be a microwave, but He is usually a crockpot. I'm on God's time, not mine. "Lord, thank you for filling my heart with patience. Lord, I give you all the praise and glory. Lord, please humble me to stay patient and wait on your will. In Jesus's name, Amen."

Last but not least, pride. I am going to tell you something maybe you didn't know.

Guess who rides shotgun with Pride?

One guess … come on. Humility is always to your right if you look. The thing about Pride is it keeps you looking in your rearview and side view mirrors. "Look what I did. I'm better than you." The only problem is that you aren't looking in the mirror, but you're looking at it. Looking in the mirror would require you to look at yourself, and not looking at yourself makes you look at other people's flaws. Today, look to the right when you get in your car.

Say these words: "Lord, may the words from my mouth, and the mediation in my heart, be acceptable in thy sight Lord. Lord, please humble me to do thy will. Please, Lord, give me a clean heart so I may serve thee. In Jesus's name, Amen."

Say it every day until you believe it. Understand sometimes God will be a crockpot, not a microwave, when you need him. I know God arrives right on time, and *GOD IS REAL, AND HE LIVES*. Humility is in everything you do and say, because you should live it.

The reward for humility and fear of the LORD is riches and honor and life."

Proverbs   22:4   ESV

"And you shall remember the whole way that the LORD your God has led you these forty years in the wilderness, that he might humble you, testing you to know what was in your heart, whether you would keep his commandments or not. And he humbled you and let you hunger and fed you with manna, which you did not know, nor did your fathers know, that he might make you know that man does not live by bread alone, but man lives by every word that comes from the mouth of the LORD."

Deuteronomy   8:2-3   ESV

AMEN.---

ABOUT THE AUTHOR

Dwight Hairston Currence resides in Charlotte, North Carolina. He loves the Lord and strives daily to inspire others to be confident in who they are. Dwight desires everyone to understand how wonderful life can be when you simply love God first and learn to let Him direct your life.

Photo credit to Doreen Tyrelle, This is Photography! Charlotte, NC

OTHER BOOKS BY AUTHOR

My Truth: 10 Days 10 Words (Paperback)
ISBN 979-8-9871031-0-4

My Truth: 10 Days 10 Words (Kindle)
ISBN 979-8-9871031-2-8

My Truth Journal
ISBN 979-8-9871031-1-1